What does an illustrator do?

Written and illustrated by

Collins

What's in this book?

Listen and say

illustrator

crayon

computer

pencil

paper

paint

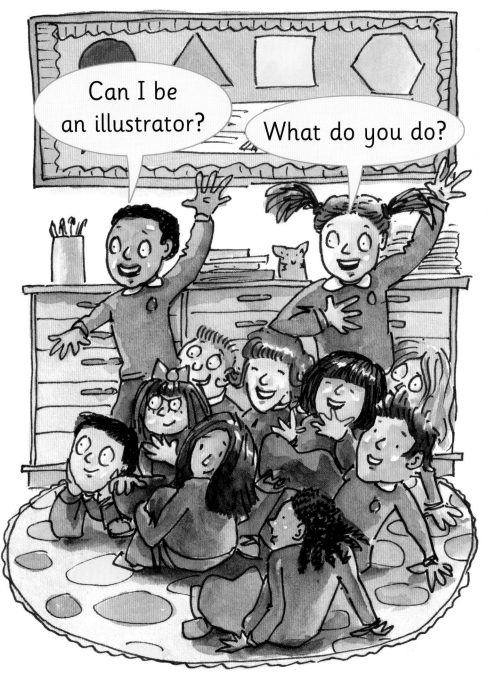

Any person can be an illustrator.

Do you like drawing pictures?

Some illustrators draw pictures for video games or films.

Some draw for comic books.

Some draw pictures for children's books.

Illustrators have lessons, so they can learn to draw.

Some go to illustrator school.

They draw and paint all day.

They learn to be an illustrator.

This is Sue. She makes books.

She needs pictures for children's books.

She asks an illustrator to draw the pictures for the story.

The illustrator draws ideas in pencil.

Sue chooses the best ideas.

The illustrator starts to draw and paint the pictures.

Some illustrators like to draw dogs best. Some like to draw trees.

Illustrators often need to see a thing to draw it.

They can look in books or on their computer.

Most illustrators work at home.
Their work room is often at the top of
the house, or at the bottom of the garden.

They try to work all day. But they walk their dogs, pick up their children from school and make the dinner, too.

Illustrators often work many hours!

Illustrators often draw and paint on paper.
They use pens and crayons, colour pencils
and paint.

Some illustrators draw on their computer.
Some pictures are difficult to draw.
Some pictures are quick and easy.

Illustrators are different.
Can you see the differences?

When the pictures are finished, they go in the book.

The book goes to shops so people can buy it and read it.

Illustrators sometimes take the books into schools and talk about them.

You can be an illustrator, too!

Draw a picture of a girl or a boy.

Start drawing in pencil.

Make a shape for the face.

Draw lines for the body and legs,

and for the shoulders and arms.

Now you can draw in pen.

Draw the eyes, nose, ears and mouth.

Make the mouth happy or sad.

Draw long hair or short hair.

Draw clothes on the body.

Now draw shoes on the feet and hands on the arms.

Write words near the mouth.

What is your person saying in the story?

Draw trees or a city behind the person.

Add cars, buses and planes.

An Illustration tells a story.

What story does your illustration tell?

Picture dictionary

Listen and repeat

buy   comic books   computer

idea   illustrator   quick

shoulder   shape

1 Look and say *"Yes"* or *"No"*

An illustrator only
uses pencils.

Illustrations go in a book.

An illustrator takes photos.

An illustrator can draw on
the computer.

2 Listen and say

Collins

Published by Collins
An imprint of HarperCollins*Publishers*
Westerhill Road
Bishopbriggs
Glasgow
G64 2QT

HarperCollins*Publishers*
1st Floor, Watermarque Building
Ringsend Road
Dublin 4
Ireland

William Collins' dream of knowledge for all began with the publication of his first book in 1819.

A self-educated mill worker, he not only enriched millions of lives, but also founded a flourishing publishing house. Today, staying true to this spirit, Collins books are packed with inspiration, innovation and practical expertise. They place you at the centre of a world of possibility and give you exactly what you need to explore it.

© HarperCollins*Publishers* Limited 2020

10 9 8 7 6 5 4 3 2

ISBN 978-0-00-839684-8

Collins® and COBUILD® are registered trademarks of HarperCollins*Publishers* Limited

www.collins.co.uk/elt

British Library Cataloguing in Publication Data

A catalogue record for this publication is available from the British Library.

Author and illustrator: Shoo Rayner
Series editor: Rebecca Adlard
Commissioning editor: Zoë Clarke
Publishing manager: Lisa Todd
Product managers: Jennifer Hall and Caroline Green
In-house editor: Alma Puts Keren
Project manager: Emily Hooton
Editor: Frances Amrani
Proofreaders: Natalie Murray and Michael Lamb
Cover designer: Kevin Robbins
Typesetter: 2Hoots Publishing Services Ltd
Audio produced by id audio, London
Reading guide author: Emma Wilkinson
Production controller: Rachel Weaver
Printed and bound by: GPS Group, SloveniaX

Download the audio for this book and a reading guide for parents and teachers at www.collins.co.uk/839684